THE JPS B'NAI MITZVAH TORAH COMMENTARY

Kedoshim (Leviticus 19:1–20:27)
Haftarah (Amos 9:7–15)

Rabbi Jeffrey K. Salkin

The Jewish Publication Society · Philadelphia
University of Nebraska Press · Lincoln

INTRODUCTION

News flash: the most important thing about becoming bar or bat mitzvah isn't the party. Nor is it the presents. Nor even being able to celebrate with your family and friends—as wonderful as those things are. Nor is it even standing before the congregation and reading the prayers of the liturgy—as important as that is.

No, the most important thing about becoming bar or bat mitzvah is sharing Torah with the congregation. And why is that? Because of all Jewish skills, that is the most important one.

Here is what is true about rites of passage: you can tell what a culture values by the tasks it asks its young people to perform on their way to maturity. In American culture, you become responsible for driving, responsible for voting, and yes, responsible for drinking responsibly.

In some cultures, the rite of passage toward maturity includes some kind of trial, or a test of strength. Sometimes, it is a kind of "outward bound" camping adventure. Among the Maasai tribe in Africa, it is traditional for a young person to hunt and kill a lion. In some Hispanic cultures, fifteen year-old girls celebrate the *quinceañera*, which marks their entrance into maturity.

What is Judaism's way of marking maturity? It combines both of these rites of passage: *responsibility* and *test*. You show that you are on your way to becoming a *responsible* Jewish adult through a public *test* of strength and knowledge—reading or chanting Torah, and then teaching it to the congregation.

This is the most important Jewish ritual mitzvah (commandment), and that is how you demonstrate that you are, truly, bar or bat mitzvah—old enough to be responsible for the mitzvot.

What Is Torah?

So, what exactly is the Torah? You probably know this already, but let's review.

The Torah (teaching) consists of "the five books of Moses," sometimes also called the *chumash* (from the Hebrew word *chameish,* which means "five"), or, sometimes, the Greek word Pentateuch (which means "the five teachings").

Here are the five books of the Torah, with their common names and their Hebrew names.

> **Genesis (The beginning), which in Hebrew is Bere'shit (from the first words—"When God began to create").** Bere'shit spans the years from Creation to Joseph's death in Egypt. Many of the Bible's best stories are in Genesis: the creation story itself; Adam and Eve in the Garden of Eden; Cain and Abel; Noah and the Flood; and the tales of the Patriarchs and Matriarchs, Abraham, Isaac, Jacob, Sarah, Rebekah, Rachel, and Leah. It also includes one of the greatest pieces of world literature, the story of Joseph, which is actually the oldest complete novel in history, comprising more than one-quarter of all Genesis.

> **Exodus (Getting out), which in Hebrew is Shemot (These are the names).** Exodus begins with the story of the Israelite slavery in Egypt. It then moves to the rise of Moses as a leader, and the Israelites' liberation from slavery. After the Israelites leave Egypt, they experience the miracle of the parting of the Sea of Reeds (or "Red Sea"); the giving of the Ten Commandments at Mount Sinai; the idolatry of the Golden Calf; and the design and construction of the Tabernacle and of the ark for the original tablets of the law, which our ancestors carried with them in the desert. Exodus also includes various ethical and civil laws, such as "You shall not wrong a stranger or oppress him, for you were strangers in the land of Egypt" (22:20).

> **Leviticus (about the Levites), or, in Hebrew, Va-yikra' (And God called).** It goes into great detail about the kinds of sacrifices that the ancient Israelites brought as offerings; the laws of ritual purity; the animals that were permitted and forbidden for eating (the beginnings of the tradition of kashrut, the Jewish dietary laws); the diagnosis of various skin diseases; the ethical laws of holiness; the ritual calendar of the Jewish year; and various agricultural laws concerning the treatment of the Land of Israel. Leviticus is basically the manual of ancient Judaism.

> Numbers (because the book begins with the census of the Isra-
  elites), or, in Hebrew, **Be-midbar (In the wilderness)**. The book
  describes the forty years of wandering in the wilderness and the
  various rebellions against Moses. The constant theme: "Egypt
  wasn't so bad. Maybe we should go back." The greatest rebellion
  against Moses was the negative reports of the spies about the
  Land of Israel, which discouraged the Israelites from wanting to
  move forward into the land. For that reason, the "wilderness generation" must die off before a new generation can come into maturity and finish the journey.

> **Deuteronomy (The repetition of the laws of the Torah), or, in
  Hebrew, Devarim (The words)**. The final book of the Torah is,
  essentially, Moses's farewell address to the Israelites as they pre-
  pare to enter the Land of Israel. Here we find various laws that
  had been previously taught, though sometimes with different
  wording. Much of Deuteronomy contains laws that will be important to the Israelites as they enter the Land of Israel—laws
  concerning the establishment of a monarchy and the ethics of
  warfare. Perhaps the most famous passage from Deuteronomy
  contains the *Shema*, the declaration of God's unity and unique-
  ness, and the *Ve-ahavta*, which follows it. Deuteronomy ends with
  the death of Moses on Mount Nebo as he looks across the Jordan
  Valley into the land that he will not enter.

Jews read the Torah in sequence—starting with Bere'shit right after Simchat Torah in the autumn, and then finishing Devarim on the
following Simchat Torah. Each Torah portion is called a parashah (di-
vision; sometimes called a *sidrah*, a place in the order of the Torah
reading). The stories go around in a full circle, reminding us that we
can always gain more insights and more wisdom from the Torah. This
means that if you don't "get" the meaning this year, don't worry—it
will come around again.

And What Else? The Haftarah

We read or chant the Torah from the Torah scroll—the most sacred
thing that a Jewish community has in its possession. The Torah is

written without vowels, and the ability to read it and chant it is part of the challenge and the test.

But there is more to the synagogue reading. Every Torah reading has an accompanying haftarah reading. Haftarah means "conclusion," because there was once a time when the service actually ended with that reading. Some scholars believe that the reading of the haftarah originated at a time when non-Jewish authorities outlawed the reading of the Torah, and the Jews read the haftarah sections instead. In fact, in some synagogues, young people who become bar or bat mitzvah read very little Torah and instead read the entire haftarah portion.

The haftarah portion comes from the Nevi'im, the prophetic books, which are the second part of the Jewish Bible. It is either read or chanted from a Hebrew Bible, or maybe from a booklet or a photocopy.

The ancient sages chose the haftarah passages because their themes reminded them of the words or stories in the Torah text. Sometimes, they chose *haftarah* with special themes in honor of a festival or an upcoming festival.

Not all books in the prophetic section of the Hebrew Bible consist of prophecy. Several are historical. For example:

The book of Joshua tells the story of the conquest and settlement of Israel.

The book of Judges speaks of the period of early tribal rulers who would rise to power, usually for the purpose of uniting the tribes in war against their enemies. Some of these leaders are famous: Deborah, the great prophetess and military leader, and Samson, the biblical strong man.

The books of Samuel start with Samuel, the last judge, and then move to the creation of the Israelite monarchy under Saul and David (approximately 1000 BCE).

The books of Kings tell of the death of King David, the rise of King Solomon, and how the Israelite kingdom split into the Northern Kingdom of Israel and the Southern Kingdom of Judah (approximately 900 BCE).

And then there are the books of the prophets, those spokesmen for God whose words fired the Jewish conscience. Their names are immortal: Isaiah, Jeremiah, Ezekiel, Amos, Hosea, among others.

Someone once said: "There is no evidence of a biblical prophet ever being invited back a second time for dinner." Why? Because the prophets were tough. They had no patience for injustice, apathy, or hypocrisy. No one escaped their criticisms. Here's what they taught:

> God commands the Jews to behave decently toward one another. In fact, God cares more about basic ethics and decency than about ritual behavior.
> God chose the Jews *not* for special privileges, but for special duties to humanity.
> As bad as the Jews sometimes were, there was always the possibility that they would improve their behavior.
> As bad as things might be now, it will not always be that way. Someday, there will be universal justice and peace. Human history is moving forward toward an ultimate conclusion that some call the Messianic Age: a time of universal peace and prosperity for the Jewish people and for all the people of the world.

Your Mission—To Teach Torah to the Congregation

On the day when you become bar or bat mitzvah, you will be reading, or chanting, Torah—in Hebrew. You will be reading, or chanting, the haftarah—in Hebrew. That is the major skill that publicly marks the becoming of bar or bat mitzvah. But, perhaps even more important than that, you need to be able to teach something about the Torah portion, and perhaps the haftarah as well.

And that is where this book comes in. It will be a very valuable resource for you, and your family, in the b'nai mitzvah process.

Here is what you will find in it:

> A brief **summary** of every Torah portion. This is a basic overview of the portion; and, while it might not refer to everything in the Torah portion, it will explain its most important aspects.
> A list of the **major ideas** in the Torah portion. The purpose: to make the Torah portion real, in ways that we can relate to. Every Torah portion contains unique ideas, and when you put all

of those ideas together, you actually come up with a list of Judaism's most important ideas.

> Two *divrei Torah* ("words of Torah," or "sermonettes") for each portion. These *divrei Torah* explain significant aspects of the Torah portion in accessible, reader-friendly language. Each *devar Torah* contains references to **traditional** Jewish sources (those that were written before the modern era), as well as **modern** sources and quotes. We have searched, far and wide, to find sources that are unusual, interesting, and not just the "same old stuff" that many people already know about the Torah portion. Why did we include these minisermons in the volume? Not because we want you to simply copy those sermons and pass them off as your own (that would be cheating), though you are free to quote from them. We included them so that you can see what is possible—how you can try to make meaning for yourself out of the words of Torah.

> **Connections:** This is perhaps the most valuable part. It's a list of questions that you can ask yourself, or that others might help you think about—any of which can lead to the creation of your *devar Torah*.

Note: you don't have to like everything that's in a particular Torah portion. Some aren't that loveable. Some are hard to understand; some are about religious practices that people today might find confusing, and even offensive; some contain ideas that we might find totally outmoded.

But this doesn't have to get in the way. After all, most kids spend a lot of time thinking about stories that contain ideas that modern people would find totally bizarre. Any good medieval fantasy story falls into that category.

And we also believe that, if you spend just a little bit of time with those texts, you can begin to understand what the author was trying to say.

This volume goes one step further. Sometimes, the haftarah comes off as a second thought, and no one really thinks about it. We have tried to solve that problem by including a **summary** of each haftarah, and then a mini-sermon on the haftarah. This will help you learn how these sacred words are relevant to today's world, and even to your own life.

All Bible quotations come from the NJPS translation, which is found in the many different editions of the JPS TANAKH; in the Conservative movement's *Etz Hayim: Torah and Commentary;* in the Reform movement's *Torah: A Modern Commentary;* and in other Bible commentaries and study guides.

How Do I Write a *Devar Torah?*

It really is easier than it looks.

There are many ways of thinking about the *devar Torah.* It is, of course, a short sermon on the meaning of the Torah (and, perhaps, the haftarah) portion. It might even be helpful to think of the *devar Torah* as a "book report" on the portion itself.

The most important thing you can know about this sacred task is: *Learn* the words. *Love* the words. Teach people what it could mean to *live* the words.

Here's a basic outline for a *devar Torah:*

"My Torah portion is (name of portion)_____ ,
    from the book of _____ , chapter

_____ .

"In my Torah portion, we learn that_____
    (Summary of portion)
"For me, the most important lesson of this Torah portion is (what
    is the best thing in the portion? Take the portion as a whole;
    your *devar Torah* does not have to be only, or specifically, on the
    verses that you are reading).
"As I learned my Torah portion, I found myself wondering:
    ➤ *Raise a question that the Torah portion itself raises.*
    ➤ *"Pick a fight"* with the portion. Argue with it.
    ➤ *Answer a question* that is listed in the "Connections" section of
      each Torah portion.
    ➤ *Suggest a question to your rabbi* that you would want the rabbi
      to answer in his or her own *devar Torah* or sermon.

"I have lived the values of the Torah by _____
(here, you can talk about how the Torah portion relates to your
own life. If you have done a mitzvah project, you can talk about
that here).

How To Keep It from Being Boring
(and You from Being Bored)

Some people just don't like giving traditional speeches. From our per-
spective, that's really okay. Perhaps you can teach Torah in a different
way—one that makes sense to you.

> Write an "open letter" to one of the characters in your Torah por-
tion. "Dear Abraham: I hope that your trip to Canaan was not too
hard . . ." "Dear Moses: Were you afraid when you got the Ten
Commandments on Mount Sinai? I sure would have been . . ."

> Write a news story about what happens. Imagine yourself to
be a television or news reporter. "Residents of neighboring cities were horrified yesterday as the wicked cities of Sodom and
Gomorrah were burned to the ground. Some say that God was
responsible . . ."

> Write an imaginary interview with a character in your Torah portion.

> Tell the story from the point of view of another character, or a mi-
nor character, in the story. For instance, tell the story of the Gar-
den of Eden from the point of view of the serpent. Or the story
of the Binding of Isaac from the point of view of the ram, which
was substituted for Isaac as a sacrifice. Or perhaps the story of
the sale of Joseph from the point of view of his coat, which was
stripped off him and dipped in a goat's blood.

> Write a poem about your Torah portion.

> Write a song about your Torah portion.

> Write a play about your Torah portion, and have some friends act
it out with you.

> Create a piece of artwork about your Torah portion.

The bottom line is: Make this a joyful experience. Yes—it could
even be fun.

The Very Last Thing You Need to Know at This Point

The Torah scroll is written without vowels. Why? Don't *sofrim* (Torah scribes) know the vowels?

Of course they do.

So, why do they leave the vowels out?

One reason is that the Torah came into existence at a time when sages were still arguing about the proper vowels, and the proper pronunciation.

But here is another reason: The Torah text, as we have it today, and as it sits in the scroll, is actually *an unfinished work*. Think of it: the words are just sitting there. Because they have no vowels, it is as if they have no voice.

When we read the Torah publicly, we give voice to the ancient words. And when we find meaning in those ancient words, and we talk about those meanings, those words jump to life. They enter our lives. They make our world deeper and better.

Mazal tov to you, and your family. This is your journey toward Jewish maturity. Love it.

THE TORAH

❖ Kedoshim: Leviticus 19:1–20:27

If you could look at the location of Parashat Kedoshim in the Torah scroll, you would notice that the parchment is pretty much evenly balanced on each side. That's because Kedoshim is the "spine" of the entire Torah. It's simply that important. Kedoshim comprises the Holiness Code, the handbook for what Jews must do in order to be a holy people.

While much of the book of Leviticus is addressed only to the priests, the text makes it clear that the Holiness Code's commandments are addressed to "the whole Israelite community." Kedoshim is the most systematic understanding of Jewish ethics to be found in the Torah, and in many places contains parallels with the Ten Commandments.

Summary

> The Israelites are to be holy, as God is holy. Through ethical and communal action, all Jews can potentially achieve holiness. (19:1–2)

> The Israelites are commanded to leave the corners of their fields unharvested, and to leave any fallen fruit for the poor and the stranger. (19:9–10)

> The commandment not to steal and not to defraud immediately leads to the commandment to pay workers on time. To not pay workers on time is the same as stealing from them. (19:13)

> It is forbidden to curse the deaf or to put a stumbling block before the blind. (19:14)

> It is forbidden to hold a grudge or to exact vengeance against people. That is one way that you will "love your neighbor [or fellow] as yourself." (19:18)

The Big Ideas

> **Holiness is one of the most precious ideas that Judaism gave to the world.** Holiness means something that is distinct, set apart, lofty. It is an attribute that "belongs" to God, but human beings can become holy in the ways that we interact with others and by the kind of society that we choose to create. Holiness, in fact, is the only quality of God to which human beings can aspire.

> **Judaism believes in *tzedakah* (righteous giving).** The Torah makes it clear that we must take care of the poor and the vulnerable in our midst, and that those actions must become public policy.

> **People should not compromise their dignity by having to wait for something that is owed to them.** That is the rationale for paying workers on time. So, too, the corners of the field "belong" to the poor; they should not have to beg for *tzedakah*.

> **Putting a stumbling block before the blind does not necessarily mean putting something in front of a blind person so that he or she will fall over it.** It is usually interpreted to mean that you should not deceive people and not take advantage of their ignorance or lack of awareness.

> **"Love your neighbor as yourself" is perhaps the best-known verse in the entire Torah, and is sometimes also known as the Golden Rule.** Some old Jewish prayer books had this commandment printed on the first page; it was considered to be the *sha'ar tefilah*, the gateway to prayer itself. But love is not primarily an emotional response to our fellow human beings. It is love in the form of action—specifically, the understanding that our neighbors are, in deep ways, just like us, and that we should treat them as we want to be treated.

Divrei Torah

GIVING IS ALL WE'VE GOT

Everyone knows that *tzedakah* is an essential Jewish value. Sooner or later, every Jew learns that the proper translation of *tzedakah* is not "charity," but "justice." There is a big difference between these two terms. "Charity" comes from the Latin word *caritas,* which means "to love." Charity, therefore, means giving as an act of love. *Tzedakah* comes from the Hebrew *tzedek,* which means "justice." It means giving because it is the right thing to do. It's a mitzvah, a commandment (not just a good deed) that you perform out of a sense of obligation, whether you are feeling "charitable" or not.

But have you ever wondered when and where the idea of *tzedakah* came from? From right here, in Parashat Kedoshim. The Torah portion actually offers the ancient Israelites two ways to do *tzedakah,* and both have to do with agriculture. The first (*peah*) is to leave the corners of the field unharvested so that the poor can help themselves. The Mishnah says: "These are the obligations without measure, whose reward lasts into eternity"—and the first item on the list is *peah.* The second is *leket,* letting the poor take anything that falls to the ground during the gleaning (harvesting) of the field.

Yes, we care about the dignity of the poor. But it's not as if you are giving away what is yours, because you don't own it in the first place! According to Jewish law, if you own a field, the corners of that field are really not yours; they belong to those who are not as fortunate as you. In fact, if you don't give to the poor, it's as if you are actually stealing from them! *Tzedakah* is the mandatory sharing of your field or your income.

Tzedakah is part of the Holiness Code; it's a way of becoming holy. It is based on the still-radical notion that you can't have it all. You don't own all your stuff (whether it's a field or money); the poor get a share of it. You don't own all of your time; Shabbat is a day of the week when you don't think about what you own (which is one good reason why traditional Jews don't go shopping on Shabbat). Ideally, on Shabbat you don't think about what you have, or about what you can consume, or about what you can buy. You think about relationships, which are themselves holy. You think about your responsibility to others, especially those in need.

The contemporary scholar and teacher Micah Goodman teaches: "The holiest word in Hebrew is a word we cannot pronounce: the four-letter Name of God, the vowels of which have disappeared. The holiest place in the world (the Holy of Holies) is a place that we cannot enter. The holy is about what is beyond you and not accessible. It is about what I cannot control."

This is perhaps the most beautiful thing about *tzedakah*. It means giving of yourself. But it also means giving up something that is part of yourself—your money, your time, your efforts. Because you don't fully own or control anything. And because God wants us to share.

Not only that: some of the happiest people you'll ever meet are those who give *tzedakah*. Try it.

THE GREATEST MITZVAH

Quick joke: A rabbi and an astronomer sat next to each other on a plane. The astronomer said to the rabbi: "I don't know much about Judaism, but wouldn't you say that the essence of Judaism is 'you shall love your neighbor as yourself'?" To which the rabbi responded: "I don't know much about astronomy, but wouldn't you say that the essence of astronomy is 'twinkle, twinkle, little star'?"

The point of the joke: one should be very careful about not oversimplifying things—including Judaism. And yet, we can forgive the astronomer for thinking that loving your neighbor is the essence of Judaism. No less an authority than the great Rabbi Akiba said: "'Love your neighbor as yourself' is the great principle [*k'lal gadol*] of the Torah."

This great principle culminates the Holiness Code in this Torah portion, and is one of the most commonly quoted verses of the entire Bible.

But wait a second. It's a commandment. How can you command someone to love? For that matter, how can you command someone to feel anything?

The clue is right there in the Hebrew. "Love your neighbor as yourself" is *ve-ahavta le-rei'akha kamokha*. Most of the time, when the Torah speaks of loving, it's more like *ve-ahavta et . . .* The *et* is a small Hebrew word indicating that the object of the sentence is coming up. Here, it's "you should love—*to* your neighbor." This doesn't even make sense. How do you love *to* someone?

That's the whole point. Love is not only a way that you feel; love is an action. Love is therefore something that you do *to* your neighbor. In fact, in the Bible, quite often *ahavah,* which means "love," doesn't really mean love as an emotion, but as a way of saying that you live in a sacred relationship with someone—that there are responsibilities. We are commanded to love the stranger, which means that we have responsibilities to him or her. We are commanded to love God, which means that we have sacred responsibilities. And, yes, our love for our neighbor is based on taking care of that person as well.

And because love is more than just a feeling, because "love" means that you have to act in certain ways, it takes practice. If you want to be a great baseball player or guitarist or dancer or artist, you have to work at it. In the same way, if you want to be a good Jew and a mensch, you have to work on it as well. Many of the mitzvot are actually part of an exercise program to make people better.

In an old *Peanuts* cartoon, Snoopy says: "I love humanity; it's people I can't stand." Martin Luther King Jr. once said of a senator who believed that blacks and whites should be completely separated: "I do not like Senator Eastland, but I must learn to love him."

The great Jewish theologian and social activist Abraham Joshua Heschel (and a friend of King) writes: "The basic dignity of man is not made up of his achievements, virtues, or special talents. It is inherent in his very being. The commandment, 'Love your neighbor as yourself' (Lev.19:18) calls upon us to love not only the virtuous and the wise, but also the vicious and the stupid person."

You love humanity, in the abstract? Great. You love your family, and your friends? Wonderful. But how are you going to love the neighbor you don't like, the classmate you don't care for, or the coworker who is a pain?

Try treating them as you would want to be treated. That's where you start.

Connections

> What is your definition of holiness? What things, places, times, and relationships are holy for you?

> What kind of *tzedakah* do you and your family support? Why are those causes important to you?

> In what ways do you try to fulfill the mitzvah of "love your neighbor"?

> Do you agree that "loving your neighbor" is a difficult commandment?

THE HAFTARAH

❖ Kedoshim: Amos 9:7–15

Judaism believes that Jews can be holy, and that's the topic of this week's Torah portion. But that doesn't mean that you are an angel, and it certainly doesn't mean that you can imagine yourself to be morally superior. The haftarah, from the book of Amos, warns us about that.

Amos was a native of Tekoa, a village south of Jerusalem, in the Southern Kingdom of Judah, who lived in the eighth century BCE. At a certain point in his life he moved to the Northern Kingdom of Israel. The Northern Kingdom was far wealthier than its southern neighbor, and the people tended to act in inappropriate ways. They were heavily into idolatry. The old Canaanite kingdom of Phoenicia was just over the border, in the territory that we call Lebanon, and elements of the ancient Canaanite religion heavily influenced the people of the Northern Kingdom. More than that, because Israel was fairly prosperous, the people there became materialistic and morally lazy.

Amos has to get the people off their high horse. He reminds them that although God made a covenant with them, God's activity is also evident in the history of other nations. And, specifically because God made a covenant with them, God will hold them responsible for all their shortcomings.

But prophetic words never end on a negative note. While Amos foresees that the kingdom of Israel will be destroyed, he also predicts that it will be rebuilt, and that this will be a sign of God's favor.

Get Over Yourselves!

"My child is special." Of course, every parent thinks that his or her child is special (and no doubt, your parents feel that way about you). But the biggest problem with "specialness" is that you might think that you are, in fact, special—and that never ends well.

That's what the prophet Amos is talking about. "To Me, O Israelites, you are just like the Ethiopians—declares the Lord. True, I brought Israel up from the land of Egypt, but also the Philistines from Caphtor and the Arameans from Kir" (9:7). In other words, God is telling the Israelites, "Get over yourselves. You are not that special."

Wait a second. Of course Israel is a special people for God. God brought them out of Egypt, right? God gave them the commandments, right? God chose them, right?

Yes, but . . .

Let's take a deeper look at what Amos is saying. "You are just like the Ethiopians." Amos is telling the people that, in God's eyes, the People of Israel are no different than a faraway people in Africa. And then God says that the Israelites shouldn't go overboard in thinking about the "specialness" of the Exodus from Egypt—because God is also present in the lives of other nations.

Take the Philistines, for example. In biblical times, they were the hereditary enemies of the nation of Israel. They were probably from Asia Minor (contemporary Turkey), and they lived on Caphtor (Crete, in the Mediterranean Sea), and God brought them out of Caphtor. And the Arameans? (The ancient Syrians, not exactly the best friends of the Israelites.) But, there again, God moved them out of Kir. God is involved with other nations as well as Israel. So much for "specialness."

The Ethiopians are sub-Saharan Africans. They are black skinned. You got a problem with that? The Talmud states, "Only one person was created at the dawn of creation, so that no one can say, 'my ancestors are better than your ancestors!'" We are all human beings with a common ancestor. Remember that.

The great sage and activist Rabbi Abraham Joshua Heschel comments: "The nations chosen for this comparison were not distinguished for might and prestige, but rather, nations which were despised and disliked. The Ethiopians were black, and in those days many of them were sold on the slave markets. The Philistines were the arch-enemies of Israel, and the Syrians continued to be a menace to the Northern Kingdom. The God of Israel is the God of all nations, and all men's history is His concern."

Rabbi Heschel was firmly committed to civil rights (he was a friend of Martin Luther King Jr. and marched with him). From that quote you can see why.

Although God has a special relationship with Israel, God also cares about other nations. Jews learn from these prophetic teachings to look at other peoples' experiences and see the similarities. The Armenians, like the Jews, have suffered exile. African Americans, like the Jews, have been persecuted. The list goes on. . . .

God lifted the Jews up again—like a fallen sukkah. And God can do the same for other peoples as well. In the meantime, we're told to lend a hand to help make it happen.

❖ Notes